D1584185

CiA Revision Series

ECDL®/ICDL® Advanced AM4 Spreadsheets

using
Microsoft® Excel

Bob Browell

Published by:

CiA Training Ltd
Business & Innovation Centre
Sunderland Enterprise Park
Sunderland SR5 2TH
United Kingdom

Tel: +44 (0) 191 549 5002
Fax: +44 (0) 191 549 9005

info@ciatraining.co.uk
www.ciatraining.co.uk

ISBN 1-86005-339-4

Release RS02v1

First published 2005

European Computer Driving Licence, ECDL and Stars Device, ECDL, International Computer Driving Licence, ICDL International Computer Driving Licence and logo, ICDL, and e-Citizen are trade marks of The European Computer Driving Licence Foundation Limited ("ECDL-F") in Ireland and other countries.

CiA Training Ltd is an entity independent of ECDL-F and is not associated with ECDL-F in any manner. This courseware publication may be used to assist candidates to prepare for AM4 Spreadsheets. Neither ECDL-F nor CiA Training Ltd warrants that the use of this courseware publication will ensure passing of AM4 Spreadsheets. Use of the ECDL-F Approved Courseware logo on this courseware publication signifies that it has been independently reviewed and approved by ECDL-F as complying with the following standard:

Technical compliance with the learning objectives of Advanced Syllabus AM4 Version 1.0

The material contained in this courseware publication has not been reviewed for technical accuracy and does not guarantee that candidates will pass AM4 Spreadsheets. Any and all assessment items and/or performance-based exercises contained in this courseware publication relate solely to this publication and do not constitute or imply certification by ECDL-F in respect of AM4 Spreadsheets or any other ECDL-F test.

For details on sitting AM4 Spreadsheets and other ECDL-F tests in your country, please contact your country's National ECDL/ICDL designated Licensee or visit ECDL-F's web site at www.ecdl.com.

Candidates using this courseware publication must be registered with the National Licensee, before undertaking AM4 Spreadsheets Without a valid registration, AM4 Spreadsheets cannot be undertaken and no ECDL/ICDL certificate, nor any other form of recognition, can be given to a candidate. Registration should be undertaken with your country's National ECDL/ICDL designated Licensee at any Approved EDCL/ICDL Test Centre.

Advanced Syllabus AM4 Version 1.0 is the official syllabus of the ECDL/ICDL certification programme at the date of approval of this courseware publication.

Approved Courseware Advanced Syllabus AM4 Version 1.0

CiA Training's **Revision Exercises** for **Advanced ECDL** contain a collection of revision exercises to provide support for students. They are designed to reinforce the understanding of the skills and techniques which have been developed whilst working through an instructional guide, such as CiA Training's *AM4 - Spreadsheets* book.

*The exercises contained within this publication are not ECDL tests. To locate your nearest ECDL test centre please go to the ECDL Foundation website at **www.ecdl.com**.*

Advanced Spreadsheets - The revision exercises cover the following topics, grouped into sections:

- Formatting
- Protection
- Cell Comments
- Names
- Templates
- Formulas
- Scenarios
- Linking
- Sorting

- Lists
- Pivot Tables
- Functions
- Charts
- Data Tables
- Macros
- Auditing
- Importing Data

A minimum of two revision exercises is included for each section. There are also general exercises, which cover techniques from any section of this guide. Answers are provided at the end of the guide wherever appropriate.

The Revision Exercises are suitable for:

- Any individual wishing to practise advanced features of this application. The user completes the exercises as required. Knowledge of *Excel* is assumed, gained for example from working through a corresponding *AM4 - Spreadsheets* book produced by **CiA**.

- Tutor led groups as reinforcement material. They can be used as and when necessary.

Aims and Objectives

To provide the knowledge and techniques necessary to be able to successfully tackle the features of an advanced word processing application. After completing the exercises the user will have experience in the following areas:

- Creating and maintaining complex spreadsheets

- Manipulating charts

- Creating and using scenarios

- Creating and using templates

- Linking cells, worksheets and workbooks

- Using complicated functions of various types

- Using data tables and databases

- Creating and using simple macros

- Using auditing techniques to check for errors.

Requirements

These revision exercises were created for *Microsoft Excel*. They assume that the computer is already switched on, that a printer and mouse are attached and that the necessary programs have been fully and correctly installed on your computer. However, in *Excel,* some features are not installed initially and a prompt to insert the *Office* CD may appear when these features are accessed.

Downloading the Data Files

The data associated with these exercises must be downloaded from our website: *www.ciatraining.co.uk/data_files*. Follow the on screen instructions to download the data files.

By default, the data files will be downloaded to **My Documents\CIA DATA FILES\Advanced ECDL Revision Series\AM4 Spreadsheets**. The data required to complete the exercises is in the **Spreadsheets Data** folder and worked solutions for every exercise can be found in the **Spreadsheets Solutions** folder.

If you prefer, the data can be supplied on CD at an additional cost. Contact the Sales team at *info@ciatraining.co.uk*.

Notation Used Throughout This Guide

- All key presses are included within < > e.g. <Enter>

- Menu selections are displayed, e.g. File | Open

- The guide is split into individual exercises. Each exercise consists of a sequential number of steps

Recommendations

- Read the whole of each exercise before starting to work through it. This ensures understanding of the topic and prevents unnecessary mistakes.

- It is assumed that the language selected is English (UK). If this is not the case select Tools | Language, select English (UK) and then the Default button.

- Some fonts used in this guide may not be available on all computers. If this is the case, select an alternative.

- Additional information and support for CiA products can be found at: www.ciasupport.co.uk, e-mail: contact@ciasupport.co.uk

The following revision exercises are divided into sections, each targeted at specific elements of the Advanced ECDL syllabus. The individual sections are an exact match for the sections in the ECDL Advanced Training Guides from CiA Training, making the guides an ideal reference source for anyone working through these exercises.

Formatting

These exercises include topics taken from the following list: freezing titles, using conditional formatting, using **AutoFormat**, using **Paste Special**.

Exercise 1

1. Open the workbook **Results**. This shows a year's operating results for a small IT Consultancy company. These need to have some new data added and some formatting applied to make the figures more readable.

2. Use **Freeze Panes** so that the row headings in column **A** are always displayed on the screen when scrolling to the right.

3. Select the range **A1:N17** and apply an **Autoformat** style of **Classic 1**.

4. The formatting is not quite acceptable. Format all the values (**B3:N17**) as currency with 2 decimal places.

5. Add italic effect to cells **A7** and **A16**. Remove the italic effect from cell **A17**.

6. Some income from maintenance contracts has been supplied on a separate workbook and needs to be included. Open the workbook **Maintenance** and copy the data (**B3:M3**).

7. Paste this data into the existing range **B6:M6** on the **Results** workbook so that only the values are pasted and these are added to any values already present. What is the new total profit for the year?

8. Apply conditional formatting to the profit values (**B17:N17**) so that any negative values are shown with a grey cell background, and all values which are not negative are shown with a pale green cell background.

9. Format row **15** (**Others**) so that it is not seen but is still included in all calculations.

10. Save the workbook as **Results2** and close it.

11. Close the **Maintenance** workbook.

Exercise 2

1. Open the workbook **Personnel**. This shows a list of Head Office staff showing their salary, date of birth and length of service in years.

2. Change the settings for the spreadsheet so that the first three rows are always displayed when scrolling down the list.

3. Apply the **AutoFormat** of **List 1** to the range **A1:G27**.

4. Change the formatting of column **G** so that the numbers appear centred horizontally in their cells.

5. Change the point size of the spreadsheet title to **14pt**.

6. Apply conditional formatting to the salary data so that any salary greater than £20,000 is displayed as **Bold** and **Italic**.

7. Apply conditional formatting so that any length of service value more than 10 years is shown with a pale yellow background and a dark blue border.

8. Return to the formatting for the salaries and add a condition to show any salary less than £12000 in a red font.

9. Highlight the range **A18:G18** and copy it to the range **A30:G30** so that the original formatting is still applied.

10. Copy it again to range **A31:G31** so that only the content is copied, i.e. none of the original formatting is applied to the copied range.

11. Save the workbook as **Personnel2** and close it.

Protection

These exercises include topics taken from the following list: protecting cells, hiding and unhiding columns and rows, creating read-only workbooks, hiding and unhiding windows, protecting workbooks.

Exercise 3

1. Open the workbook **Secure**. The is a payroll workbook which has been password protected. Use the password **pass** to access the file.

2. The worksheet is to be given to data entry personnel to enter the weekly figures, so you need to remove the password security. Save the workbook as **Secure2**, first removing the password protection.

3. To check that the password has been removed, close the workbook, **Secure2** and then reopen it.

4. **Robson** is on temporary assignment to another plant. Zero his hourly rate (**H2**), then hide the whole of column **H**.

5. Hide row **2**.

6. The data entry personnel will only be allowed to enter the number of hours worked. Remove the cell protection from the range **B4:J4**.

7. Apply worksheet protection, using a password **sheet**.

8. Verify the protection. Attempt to change the number of hours worked for **Asif** to **50**. What is the effect?

9. Attempt to change the overtime rate (**B16**) to **2.0**. What is the effect?

10. Attempt to unhide row **2**. What is the effect?

11. What action would be necessary before row **2** could be unhidden?

12. Save the workbook with its existing name (**Secure2**) overwriting the previous save, and close it.

Exercise 4

1. Open the workbook **Cars**. This shows car sales statistics from a dealer, analysed by colour.

2. Give 2 ways you might tell that there is another (hidden) sheet in this workbook.

3. Display the hidden worksheet, **Data**. Display the hidden column on this sheet.

4. Apply worksheet protection to the whole of the **Analysis** sheet so that no amendments can be made.

5. Apply worksheet protection to the **Data** sheet such that data can only be entered in the range **B3:G15**.

6. Enter some typical data for week **6 (B8:G8)**.

7. The **Analysis** sheet is protected, so will the values change to reflect the new data in **Data**?

8. Save the workbook as **Cars2**, with a **Password to modify** of **pass**.

9. Close the workbook.

10. Open the workbook **Cars2**. What options are offered as it opens?

11. Open the workbook as **Read Only**.

12. Attempt to add some more data for week 7 on the **Data** sheet. Is this allowed?

13. Attempt to save the workbook with the same name. Is this allowed?

14. Cancel the save and close the workbook without saving.

Cell Comments

These exercises include topics taken from the following list: using cell comments, displaying comments, creating, editing and deleting comments.

Exercise 5

1. Open the workbook **Business** showing a business plan. You need to review the figures and add comments so that it can be sent back to the Finance Department.

2. Add the comment **These figures MUST be reduced** to cell **B10**.

3. Add the comment **By how much can we increase this?** to cell **B16**.

4. Add the comment **We don't make a profit until June! This is not good enough!** to cell **G12**.

5. Move all of the comments so that none of them covers any of the spreadsheet data when using **View | Comments**.

6. Print a copy of the spreadsheet (in landscape orientation) showing the comments in their correct locations.

7. The comment in **G12** is not particularly helpful. Delete it.

8. Print a copy of the spreadsheet with the comments shown at the end of the sheet.

9. Amend the spreadsheet so that the comment markers are shown but the actual comments are not displayed.

10. Save the workbook as **Business2** and close it.

Exercise 6

1. Open the workbook **Wages** showing proposed salary increases. The Managing Director has added some comments.

2. Move the cursor over each comment to read them.

3. Delete the third comment (**F17**).

4. Use a menu command to show all comments in their correct positions. What is the command?

5. Change the text colour in the first comment to red.

6. By clicking on the border of the second comment, change the background colour to pale blue.

7. In the final comment, add your initials and the text **Regrading due next month**.

8. Print a copy of the spreadsheet (in landscape orientation) showing the comments in their correct locations.

9. Save the workbook as **Wages2** and close it.

Names

These exercises include topics taken from the following list: using names, creating names from ranges, pasting and applying names, using names in formulas, using names with **Go To**.

Exercise 7

1. Open the workbook **Payroll**. This shows the payroll calculations for a small department.

2. Click in cell **B14** and **Define** a name of **NI**. Similarly define names of **TAX**, and **OT** for cells **B15**, and **B16**.

3. Create names for the main part of the worksheet, i.e. **A1:K11**, then apply all names (including **NI**, **TAX**, and **OT**).

4. What is the formula now for **Basic Pay** in cell **B6**?

5. What is the formula now for **National Insurance** in cell **B9**?

6. Move to cell **B18** and type **=Gross_Pay Patel** to find the value of gross pay for **Patel**. Format the cell as currency. What is the gross pay?

7. What expression needs to be typed in cell **B19** to display the **Basic Pay** for **Fisher**?

8. A new pension scheme is proposed and it is required to calculate what the contributions will be. Enter **Pension Rate** in **A17** and **5%** in **B17**.

9. Define a name of **Pension** for cell **B17**.

10. In **A12** enter **New Pension**.

11. In **B12** use the **Paste Name** feature to enter a formula multiplying gross pay by the pension rate.

12. Copy the formula into **C12** to **K12** and format the range **B12** to **K12** as currency. What is the total pension contribution?

13. Save the workbook as **Payroll2** and close it.

Exercise 8

1. Open the workbook **Growth**. This is the business plan for a small manufacturing company where the number of units sold and the number of employees is estimated to grow at a certain rate.

2. Define a name of **Rate** for cell **B15**.

3. Apply this name to the spreadsheet data, **A2:N12**.

4. What is the formula for the units sold in May (**F3**)?

5. Create names for the whole spreadsheet data area **A2:N12** in a single operation. Base the names on the top row and the left column.

6. Apply these names to the same area.

7. What is the new formula for the units sold in May (**F3**)?

8. What is the formula for the May costs (**F11**)?

9. Go to the range of cells named **Costs** and apply a background colour of pale blue.

10. Highlight the range **N3:N12**. What name appears in the **Name Box** to the left of the **Formula Bar**?

11. Save the workbook as **Growth2** and close it.

Templates

These exercises include topics taken from the following list: creating and understanding templates, using templates, editing templates, deleting templates.

Exercise 9

1. Start a new workbook and enter the following labels and formulas.

	A	B	C
1	Time Sheet		
2			
3	Day	Hours	Hours to Pay
4	Monday		=B4
5	Tuesday		=B5
6	Wednesday		=B6
7	Thursday		=B7
8	Friday		=B8
9	Saturday		=B9*1.5
10	Sunday		=B10*2
11	TOTAL	=SUM(B4:B10)	=SUM(C4:C10)
12			
13	Hourly Rate		
14	Attendance Bonus		=IF(B11>20,25,0)
15			
16	Weekly Pay		=(C11*B13)+C14
17			

   C9 Saturday paid at time and a half

   C10 Sunday paid at double time

   C14 Bonus of £25 paid if over 20 hours are worked

2. Format cells **B13**, **C14** and **C16** as **Currency** with **2** decimal places.

3. Save the workbook as a template named **Time** (in the **Templates** folder).

4. Save the workbook again, this time as a template named **Time** in your data folder.

5. Close the workbook.

6. Start a new workbook and base it on the template **Time**, which should now exist as one of the available templates in *Excel*.

7. Enter details for someone who has worked exactly **4** hours every day of the week, at an hourly rate of **£5**. What is that person's weekly pay?

8. Print a copy of the whole worksheet then save the workbook as **Timesheet** and close it.

9. Delete the template **Time** from the **Templates** folder. Leave the copy which is in your data folder.

Exercise 10

1. Open the workbook **Plan**. This worksheet is to be used to create a template to be used to create different models of a manufacturing company.

2. Delete the contents of **B3**, **B6**, **B15** and **B16**.

3. Delete the ranges **B7:M7** and **B10:M10**. There should be no non-zero values remaining in the spreadsheet.

4. Save the workbook as a template named **Plantemp** (in the **Templates** folder).

5. Save the workbook again, this time as a template named **Plantemp** in your data folder.

6. Close the workbook.

7. Start a new workbook and base it on the template **Plantemp**, which should now exist as one of the available templates in *Excel*.

8. Enter units sold in January (**B3**) as **500**, and enter employees in January (**B6**) as **10**.

9. Enter **1000** in the range **B7:M7** (**Pay**), and **9000** in the range **B10:M10** (**Overheads**).

10. Enter a Growth Rate of **4%** (**B15**) and a Unit Price of **45** (**B16**).

11. The model is now complete. What is the **Net Profit** figure for the year based on these figures?

12. Save the workbook as **Plan2** and close it.

13. Delete the template **Plantemp** from the **Template** folder. Leave the copy which is in your data folder.

Formulas

These exercises include topics taken from the following list: displaying and checking formulas, understanding formulas that produce errors, creating custom number formats.

Exercise 11

1. Open the workbook **Office**. This shows the calculated salary increases for some office personnel and their pension scheme account numbers. The spreadsheet contains some errors however and these need to be corrected before the information can be passed on for approval.

2. Identify and correct the error in row **6**.

3. Identify and correct the error in row **10**.

4. Identify and correct the error in row **14**.

5. Why is it not necessary to correct the errors in row **27**, the total line?

6. The pension scheme account numbers must all have 6 digits and have a dash between the first and last three-digit groups. Use **Custom** format to ensure that all numbers in column **H** conform to this rule. What entry is made in the **Custom** format type to achieve this?

7. Save the workbook as **Office2** and close it.

Exercise 12

1. Open the workbook **Fruit**. This has been prepared to show the sales performance of a fruit stall in the market for the first quarter of the year, but unfortunately it contains some errors.

2. Identify and correct the errors in row **8**.

3. What is the most likely cause of the errors in row **8**?

4. Identify and correct the errors in row **13**.

5. Use **Custom** format to display the date in **A16** as **Sat 17 Apr 2004**.

6. Display the spreadsheet so that all formulas are visible.

7. Print a copy of the spreadsheet using this display in **Landscape** orientation.

8. Save the workbook as **Fruit2** and close it.

Scenarios

These exercises include topics taken from the following list: creating scenarios, using and editing scenarios, creating scenario summary reports.

Exercise 13

1. Open the workbook **Company**. This is the business plan for a small manufacturing company where the number of units sold and the number of employees is estimated to grow at a certain rate. The sales price of a unit can also be varied.

2. Use the **Scenario Manager** to add a scenario named **Base**, where the changing cells are **B15** and **B16** and they have values of **5%** and **7**.

3. Add another scenario named **Bad News** where the growth rate, **B15**, has dropped to **3%**.

4. Add another scenario named **Recovery** with a growth rate of **3%** and a sales price of **7.2** per unit.

5. To see the effect of lowering prices and achieving higher sales growth, add a scenario named **Cheap** with a sales price of **6.5** and a growth rate of **8%**.

6. Finally add a scenario named **Hopeful** where the growth rate is **8%** and the sales price is **7**.

7. Show each of the scenarios and determine which one results in the biggest loss.

8. Create a **Scenario Summary** based on these scenarios with a **Result Cell** of **N12**.

9. Delete the **Cheap** scenario.

10. Save the workbook as **Company2** and close it.

Exercise 14

1. Open the workbook **NewSalaries**. This shows the planned salary increases for the staff in the head office of a company. The new salaries are based on a percentage increase (shown in cell **E31**) and a fixed amount increase (shown in **E32**).

2. Create a scenario based on the current values in **E31** and **E32**. Name the scenario **Medium**.

3. Add a scenario **High Amount**, based on values of **2%** and **£1300**.

4. Add a scenario **High Rate**, based on values of **6%** and **£500**.

5. Show each of the scenarios and determine which one results in the lowest increase in the total salary bill.

6. Create a **Scenario Summary** based on these scenarios, showing **Result Cells** of **G27** (total increase), **G28** (minimum increase) and **G29** (maximum increase).

7. Which scenario results in the greatest spread of increase percentages, i.e. the greatest difference between the minimum and maximum percentages? What is the spread?

8. Print the summary spreadsheet.

9. Save the workbook as **NewSalaries2** and close it.

Linking

These exercises include topics taken from the following list: linking cells, linking between worksheets, linking between workbooks, linking to a word document, consolidation using 3D-sum.

Exercise 15

1. Open the workbook **Bits**. This shows the operating results for a company with plants in three locations. The figures for each plant are shown on a separate sheet, but to ensure consistency, the figures to be used in the costing calculations are held on a single sheet, **Central**.

2. On the **Newtown** sheet, enter a formula in **C8** to calculate the production costs. This is the **Number of Units** for Newtown multiplied by the **Production Cost per Unit** from the **Central** sheet.

3. On the **Newtown** sheet, enter a formula in **C9** to calculate the overhead costs. This is the **Employees** figure for Newtown multiplied by the **Overhead Cost per Employee** from the **Central** sheet.

4. On the **Newtown** sheet, enter a formula in **C10** to show the portion of the Head Office costs allocated to Newtown. This figure is held directly on the **Central** sheet.

5. Enter similar formulas on the **Oldfield** and **Concord** sheets.

6. The formulas to calculate the profit figures for each individual plant have already been entered. Which plant shows a loss?

7. On the **Central** sheet, the consolidated profit for all plants is to be shown in cell **C12**. Use a **SUM** function in **C12** to total the profit figures from each individual sheet. What is the formula and the calculated value?

8. The production cost per unit has been underestimated. On the **Central** sheet, change this value to **82**. What is the new Consolidated Profit?

9. Print one copy of the each of the four sheets in the workbook.

10. Save the workbook as **Bits2** and then close it.

Exercise 16

1. Open the workbook **Horseshoes**. The **Bookings** sheet shows the bookings taken for the various room types in the Three Horseshoes Inn. The **Occupancy** sheet will calculate the overall percentage occupancy of each room type for inclusion in a report.

2. Use the **Copy/Paste Link** feature to create a link in cell **C5** on the **Occupancy** sheet to read the value in cell **N3** on the **Bookings** sheet.

3. Similarly, create links in **D5**, **E5** and **F5** on the **Occupancy** sheet, to the appropriate totals on the **Bookings** sheet.

4. The calculations for percentage occupancy are already in place. Which room type has the lowest occupancy percentage?

5. In *Word*, open the document **Report**. Copy the range **B3:F6** from the **Occupancy** worksheet and paste it as a link after the text in the document.

6. Print a copy of the document.

7. Save a copy of the document as **Report53** and close it.

8. Close *Word*.

9. Save the workbook as **Horseshoes2** and then close it.

Sorting

These exercises include topics taken from the following list: sorting data, performing multiple sorts, performing custom sorts, subtotals.

Exercise 17

1. Open the workbook **Staff**.

2. Sort the data by **Date of Birth** so that the youngest person is shown first. What sort direction is this?

3. Now sort the data so that the oldest person is shown first. Who is the oldest person on the spreadsheet?

4. Perform a multiple sort on the data, first by **Department** (alphabetically), then by **Date of Birth** (oldest first). Who is the oldest person in the Computer Services Department?

5. Add subtotals so that salaries are summed for each department. Show the subtotals below each block of data. What is the total salary for the Computer Services Department?

6. Replace these subtotals with new ones which show the average length of service for each department. What is the average length of service for the Development Department? To the nearest year, what is the overall average length of service for the company?

7. Change the text for the **Grand Average** to **Company Average**.

8. Change the display so that only the subtotals are shown.

9. Display the detail lines for the **Finance** department only.

10. Print the **Finance** department details.

11. Save the workbook as **Staff2** and close it.

Exercise 18

1. Open the workbook **Events** which lists the main events scheduled for a forthcoming convention. This needs to be turned into a timetable.

2. Perform a multiple sort on the data, first by **Day** and then by **Time**. For the sort by **Day**, use the **Sort Options** to cause the data to be sorted in the order Monday, Tuesday, etc. For the sort by **Time** use the normal Ascending option.

3. Apply subtotals on each change of **Day** to show the starting (Minimum) time. Show the subtotals above the data.

4. Delete the row containing the **Grand Min**.

5. Change the **Monday Min** title to **Monday Start**. Change all the other subtotal titles appropriately and widen column **D** if necessary.

6. Print a copy of the timetable.

7. Save the workbook as **Events2** and close it.

Lists

These exercises include topics taken from the following list: creating a list, filtering lists using the **AutoFilter**, using custom criteria with **AutoFilter**, using the advanced filter, filtering using complex criteria, extracting filtered data.

Section Exercises

Exercise 19

1. Open the workbook **Stock**. This is the stock list for the bar in a small restaurant.

2. Insert a new column before **Order Quantity**. In **F4** add a title of **Weeks Stock**.

3. In **F5:F58** add a formula to divide **Stock Quantity** by **Weekly Turnover**. Format the values as **Numeric** with **2** decimal places.

4. Use **Autofilter** to display the **Beers** only. How many items are classed as beers?

5. Show all records then use **Custom Autofilter** to display items with a weekly turnover of at least **100**. How many items are selected?

6. Use **Autofilter** to display the **Top Ten** items by turnover. How many of these items are classed as beers?

7. You need to generate an order to the company supplying your beers. Use Advanced Filter to list items with a type of **Beers** and **Weeks Stock** value less than **1**. Use rows **2** and **3** for the filter criteria and show the filtered items as a new list starting in **A62**.

8. Highlight the new list (**A61:G65**) and print out only the selected cells.

9. Save the workbook as **Stock2** and close it.

Exercise 20

1. Open the workbook **Employees**.

2. Use **Autofilter** to display staff in the **Development** department. How many are there?

3. Show all records then use **Autofilter** to display the top five highest paid employees. How many of these employees are in the marketing department?

4. Use **Custom Autofilter** to display <u>all</u> staff born before 1960. How many staff are selected?

5. You need to identify a very specific group of employees. Use **Advanced Filter** to list employees who have more than 5 years service and a salary between £15000 and £20000. How many staff are selected?

6. This is too selective. Amend the filter criteria to also include anyone born before 1964. How many staff are now selected?

7. Print the list, including the selection criteria.

8. Save the workbook as **Employees2** and close it.

Pivot Tables

These exercises include topics taken from the following list: understanding pivot tables, creating a pivot table, updating a pivot table, grouping data in a pivot table.

Exercise 21

1. Open the workbook **Analysis**.

2. Amend the heading in column **G** to **Service**.

3. Create a pivot table based on the entire list, using the following specification:

Location	**New sheet**
Row Field	**Department**
Column Field	**Service**
Data Items	**Count of Surname**

4. Change the name of the worksheet containing the pivot table to **Pivot**.

5. According to the pivot table, how many staff have exactly 4 years service?

6. There has been a reorganisation; the **Finance** department has been absorbed into administration. On the original data spreadsheet (**Sheet1**) change the employees of the **Finance** department to **Administration**.

7. Refresh the data in the pivot table

8. According to the pivot table, how many staff are now in the **Administration** department?

9. The **Marketing** department is not to be included in this analysis. Amend the pivot table so that data for that department is not shown on the table.

10. Change the layout of the pivot table so that **Department** is the column field and **Service** is the row field.

11. Apply any of the **Table** style **AutoFormats**.

12. Save the workbook as **Analysis2** and close it.

Exercise 22

1. Open the workbook **Goods**.

2. Create a pivot table based on the entire list, using the following specification:

Location	**New sheet**
Row Field	**Type**
Column Field	**none**
Data Items	**Sum of Weekly Turnover**

3. Print a copy of the pivot table.

4. Delete the sheet containing the pivot table.

5. Create another pivot table based on the entire list, using the following specification:

Location	**New sheet**
Row Field	**Type**
Column Field	**Weekly Turnover**
Data Items	**Count of Items**

6. Switch the Row and Column fields.

7. Remove the **Miscellaneous** type records from the table.

8. Group the **Weekly Turnover** values in column **A** into the following groupings:

   1 - 10
   11- 50
   51 - 100
   Over 100

9. Use the range definitions above as the group names.

10. Hide all detail.

11. Apply any of the **Table** style **AutoFormats**.

12. Print the pivot table.

13. Save the workbook as **Goods2** and close it.

Functions

These exercises include topics taken from the following list: using logical functions, using date and time functions, using lookup functions, using maths and financial functions, using text functions, using database functions, using nested functions.

Exercise 23

1. Open the workbook **Holidays**.

2. Total all the salaries in cell **E27**.

3. Enter **Higher Salaries** in **D29** and **Lower Salaries** in **D30**.

4. Without making any other changes to the worksheet, add a function in **E29** to sum all salaries in the range **E4:E26** that are greater than **17000**, and add a function in **F29** to count all the salaries that make up that total.

5. Similarly, add a function in **E30** to sum all salaries in the range **E4:E26** that are less than or equal to **17000**, and add a function in **F30** to count all the salaries that make up that total.

6. Add **E29** and **E30** and check that the sum is the same as the grand total in **E27**.

7. Enter the following table of holiday entitlements starting in **D34**:

Service	0	5	10
Holidays	20	25	30

8. In **H3** add the heading **Holidays** and make sure it has the same format as the other titles.

9. In **H4** add a function to lookup the holiday entitlement for this employee from the data in **E34:G35**.

10. Copy the function to the range **H5:H26**.

11. In **I3** add the heading **Increase** and make sure it has the same format as the other titles.

12. In **I4** add a function to calculate the salary increase. This is based on an increase of **4%** (0.04) for salaries over £**17000**, and **5%** (0.05) for all others.

13. Copy the function to the range **I5:I26** and format the range as currency.

14. What is the holiday entitlement and salary increase for **Anna Li**?

15. Save the workbook as **Holidays2** and close it.

Exercise 24

1. Open the workbook **Debts**. This is a list of a company's outstanding debts which needs analysis.

2. Enter a date of **01/09/03** in **E1**.

3. Enter a heading of **OVERDUE** in **H4**.

4. Enter a calculation in **H5** to show the number of days between the date in **E1**, and the invoice due date in **B5**.

5. Make the reference to **E1** an absolute address then copy the formula to **H6:H49**.

6. Use a database function in **C51** to count the number of invoices which are <u>not</u> scheduled (represented by a value of **FALSE** in the **Scheduled** column) and are more than **30** days overdue. Use rows 2 and 3 for the selection criteria. Format **C51** as **Numeric** with no decimal places. What is the answer and the formula?

7. Use a database function in **C52** to sum the values of the invoices which are <u>not</u> scheduled and are more than **30** days overdue.

8. Format the cell **C52** as **Currency** with no decimal places.

9. The company cannot afford to pay that much. Change the selection criteria for the two calculations to include only invoices which are <u>not</u> scheduled and are more than **45** days overdue. What are the new totals?

10. The invoices to pay must be marked. Enter the label **TO PAY** in cell **I4**. Add a nested logical function in **I5** to display the text **PAY** if Scheduled is **FALSE** and Overdue is greater than **45** days, otherwise display a blank cell.

11. Copy the formula to **I6:I49**.

12. Enter the label **CONTACT** in cell **J4**. Format the two new labels the same as the other labels in the row.

13. In the cell **J5** add a <u>function</u> to display the **First Name** and **Surname** (separated by a space) for the Tip Top Travel contact (Yvonne Dawson).

14. Copy the formula to **J6:J49**.

15. What function would you need to enter in **E1** if you wanted the date used in the calculations to be automatically the current date (with no time display)?

16. Save the workbook as **Debts2** and close it.

Charts

These exercises include topics taken from the following list: formatting charts, modifying charts, inserting images in 2D charts.

Exercise 25

1. Open the workbook **Tokyo**. This shows the Rainfall and Temperature data in Tokyo for one year. A chart of the data is shown in the worksheet **Chart**.

2. On the **Chart** sheet, move the title down so that it is in the top left of the plot area, and increase the font size of the title to **14pt**. Move the **Legend** into the **Plot Area**.

3. Format the **Plot Area** to have a gradient colour effect using the two colours **Light Turquoise** and **Aqua**.

4. Format the text on both axes to be **Bold** and **Italic**.

5. Change the chart type for the **Temperature** data series to be a **Line** chart with markers. Format the line as dark red.

6. Print a copy of the chart.

7. Remove the **Temperature** data series from the chart.

8. Amend the chart title to **Tokyo Rainfall**.

9. Format the **Rainfall** data series to have a **Gap Width** of **50** and a **Texture Fill Effect** of **Water Droplets**.

10. Format the **Plot Area** to be filled with the **Rain.gif** image from the data files.

11. Print a copy of the chart.

12. Switch the **Plot Area** and **Data Series** fill effects. That is, apply the **Water Droplets** fill effect to the **Plot Area**, and the **Rain.gif** image to the **Data Series** (use the **Stack** format).

13. Print a copy of the chart.

14. Save the workbook as **Tokyo2** and close it.

Exercise 26

1. Open the workbook **Sales**. This shows car sales from a dealer, analysed by colour.

2. Highlight the ranges **B3:H3** and **B6:H6** then use the Chart Wizard to create a 2D bar chart based on these values. Display the chart on a separate worksheet named **Chart**.

3. Change the chart type to an **Exploded Pie** chart.

4. Format the **Plot Area** to have no background colour and no border.

5. Format the **Data Series** so that the **Data Labels** show both **Category name** and **Percentage** (**Label and percent** in *Excel97*).

6. Format each **Data Point** (Segment) to have the fill colour to match its label. For the **Silver** segment, there is a suitable effect listed under the Preset Colours in the **Gradient** fill effects. For the **Other** segment, use your imagination, possibly a **Pattern** effect may be appropriate.

7. Remove the **Legend** from the chart as it is no longer necessary.

8. Change the chart title to **New Sales Colour Split** and format it as **Arial 14pt**. Move it closer to the chart segments.

9. Format the **Data Labels** to be **Bold** and **Italic**.

10. Print a copy of the **Chart** worksheet.

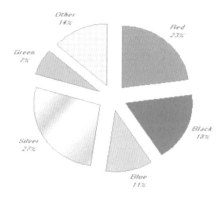

11. Save the workbook as **Sales2** and close it.

Data Tables

These exercises include topics taken from the following list: creating a one input data table, creating a two input data table.

Exercise 27

1. Open the workbook **Starship**. The top speed of a Federation Starship depends on its mass and the number of dilithium crystals in the main drive. The formula for the top speed has been entered in **B10**, based on the values for the number of crystals (**D5**) and the starship mass in kilotons (**D7**). This data needs to be displayed as a table for a range of different values.

2. In the range **C10:H10** enter the series of numbers, **10**, **20**, **30**, **40**, **50**, **60** to represent the range of possible starship masses.

3. In the range **B11:B20** enter the series of numbers, **6** to **15**, to represent the possible values for the number of crystals used.

4. Copy the formatting from **B10** to both the ranges just added.

5. Create a two input data table in the range **B10:H20**.

6. Starship speeds are always quoted to the nearest whole number, e.g. Warp factor 5, so format the range **B10:H20** as **Numeric** with **0** decimal places.

7. What is the top speed of a **20** kiloton ship with a **12** crystal drive?

8. A negative or zero speed means that the drive is not powerful enough to move the ship at all. What is the minimum number of crystals to use so that a 60 kiloton ship can be moved?

9. Save the workbook as **Starship2** and close it.

Exercise 28

1. Open a new workbook. You are going to create a table to show the profitability of running 20 seater minibus trips to a local night club, including admission charges. There are fixed costs of £400 for the enterprise which must be paid regardless of the number of people attending. The profitability is calculated from the Number of

Passengers multiplied by Ticket Price, minus the fixed costs. An estimated acceptable price is thought to be **£25**.

2. In **B2** enter **Passengers** , in **B3** enter **Ticket Price** and in **B4** enter **Costs**. Widen column **B** to show all titles.

3. As a sample, in **C2** enter **10**, in **C3** enter **25**, and in **C4** enter **400**.

4. In **B7** enter the formula to calculate the profitability, **=C2*C3-C4**.

5. Enter the numbers **10** to **20** in the range **B8:B18**. This represents the number of passengers on the bus.

6. In the range **C7:H7** enter the value **£25** to **£50** in **£5** steps to represent the ticket prices.

7. Create a two input data table in the range **B7:H18** to calculate the profitability of the enterprise.

8. Format the data range **C8:H18** as currency, zero decimal places, with negative numbers shown in red with a minus sign.

9. From the table, how many passengers are needed at **£25** a ticket to create a profit?

10. If a minimum of 12 passengers can be guaranteed, what ticket price will be needed to guarantee a profit?

11. With the minimum of 12 passengers still guaranteed and the fixed costs cut to **£350** (amend the value in **C4**), could the ticket price be reduced to **£30** and still guarantee not to lose money?

12. Print a copy of the table.

13. Save the workbook as **Minibus** and close it.

Macros

These exercises include topics taken from the following list: understanding macros, recording a macro, running a macro, assigning a macro to a button on a toolbar.

Exercise 29

1. Open the workbook **Inn**.

The Three Horseshoes Inn

2. Make sure the **Occupancy** sheet is active and click in cell **C1**.

3. Start recording a new macro. Name the macro **Stamp**, assign a shortcut key of **Ctrl q** and store the macro in this workbook.

4. When the macro is recording click the **Italic** formatting button.

5. Type **Property of CiA Training** and press **<Enter>**.

6. Stop recording the macro.

7. Edit the macro **Stamp**.

8. From the **Visual Basic** window select **File | Print** to obtain a printout of the macro code. Close the **Visual Basic** window.

9. Switch to the **Bookings** sheet.

10. Click in cell **K8** and run the **Stamp** macro with a key press.

11. Delete the **Stamp** macro.

12. Save the workbook as **Inn2** and close it.

Exercise 30

1. Open the workbook **Vehicles**.

2. Click in cell **A1** of the **Analysis** sheet and record a new macro.

3. Name the macro **Special**, assign a shortcut key of **Ctrl f** and store the macro in this workbook.

4. Record the macro to set the font to **Comic Sans MS**, **11pt**, **Bold** and dark blue, then stop recording.

5. Unhide the **Data** worksheet.

6. Run the special macro on cell **A1** of the **Data** sheet.

7. Switch back to the **Analysis** sheet and record a new macro with a name of **Output**. Make sure the macro is stored with this workbook.

8. The macro is to set **Landscape** page orientation, centre the worksheet horizontally and vertically on the printed page, and request **Gridlines** to be included in the print.

9. Create a new button on the **Formatting** toolbar and assign the **Output** macro to it. Change the name of the button to **Output**.

10. Save the workbook as **Vehicles2**.

11. Remove the **Output** button from the toolbar.

12. Close **Vehicles2** <u>without</u> saving.

13. If you were to open **Vehicles2** now, would the **Output** macro and the **Output** button still be available?

Revision Series
© CiA Training Ltd 2005

Auditing

These exercises include topics taken from the following list: using auditing tools, tracing precedents and dependents, adding and removing tracer arrows, tracing errors.

Exercise 31

1. Open the workbook **Preliminary**. This shows the calculated salary increases for some office personnel. Data validation has been applied to columns **E** and **H**. Some formula errors and invalid data are present.

2. Use a command to display red circles around all cells with invalid data. How many cells are circled?

3. What is the name of the toolbar which contains the command necessary for step 2? How many buttons are on that toolbar?

4. Clear all validation circles.

5. Display the precedents of cell **G5**.

6. Display the precedents of cell **G6**. How do they differ from **G5**?

7. Remove all precedent arrows.

8. Trace the dependants of **E32** (the salary increase percentage). Is it applied in all of the new salary calculations in column **F**?

9. Remove all dependant arrows

10. Use an **Auditing** toolbar button to trace the errors in **G27**.

11. According to the trace, what is the immediate cause of the error in **G27**?

12. What is the immediate cause of the error in **F27**?

13. Trace the error.

14. Print the selection **A13:G33**.

15. Save the workbook as **Preliminary2** and close it.

Exercise 32

1. Open the workbook **Manufacturing**. This shows the results from 3 manufacturing plants, using some values obtained from a **Central** worksheet. The overall results are then consolidated onto the **Central** sheet.

2. It is suspected that the workbook is giving incorrect results. View each of the worksheets. There are no errors indicated, so all the formulas are valid, although they may not all be correct.

3. Using buttons from the **Formula Auditing** toolbar, trace the precedents for the **Profit** calculation (**C12**) on the **Newtown**, **Oldfields** and **Concord** sheets. Which one is different from the others?

4. Correct all of the incorrect formula.

5. On the **Central** sheet, trace the dependants for **Production Cost per Unit**, **C5**. Is it used consistently in the correct cell (**C8**) on all 3 subsidiary sheets? If not, correct any errors.

6. On the **Central** sheet, trace the dependants for **Overhead Cost per Employee**, **C6**. Is it used consistently in the correct cell (**C9**) on all 3 subsidiary sheets? If not, correct any errors.

7. On the **Central** sheet, trace the precedents for **Consolidated Profit**, **C12**. Does it include the correct cells (**C12**) from all 3 subsidiary sheets. If not, correct the formula.

8. What is the new **Consolidated Profit** value?

9. Save the workbook as **Manufacturing2** and close it.

Importing Data

These exercises include topics taken from the following list: importing delimited text.

Exercise 33

1. Open the workbook **Invoices** and. This will be the list of outstanding invoices for a plumbing supplies company for the months of January and February. All that is missing is the data.

2. Make sure the **January** sheet is displayed and import the text file **Raw data.txt** so that it starts in cell **A3**.

3. The file is delimited, the **Delimiter** is **Comma** and the **Text qualifier** should be ".

4. Do not apply any extra formatting and make sure the imported data will be put in the existing worksheet.

5. Enter **Totals** in **D14** and make it **Bold**.

6. Use **Autosum** in **E14**, **F14** and **G14** to total the appropriate columns.

7. Format all the data and totals in columns **E**, **F** and **G** to be currency with 2 decimal places. Increase the width of all columns so that all data is visible.

8. What is the total invoice amount including Tax?

9. Format all dates in the style **10-Jan-2003**. Widen the column if necessary.

10. Switch to the **February** worksheet and Import the text file **Raw data2.txt** so that it starts in cell **A3**. This file is tab delimited.

11. Apply all the same totalling and formatting that was used in the **January** sheet.

12. Save the workbook as **Invoices2** and close it.

Exercise 34

1. Open a new workbook.

2. Enter the headings **Number**, **Surname**, **First Name**, **Department**, **Absence** in the cells **A1:E1**.

3. Make the headings **Bold** and **Italic**.

4. Position the cursor in cell **A2** and import the text file **AbsenceNorth.txt**. This is the data from the Northern Office of a company showing how many days absence each employee has registered.

5. The file is **Tab** delimited, no extra formatting is required and the imported data should be placed in the **Existing worksheet** at location **$A$2**.

6. The data from the Southern Office has also been received in a text file **AbsenceSouth.txt**. Import this data onto the same worksheet starting in location **A13**.

7. Widen columns so that all data and headings can be seen.

8. Sort the data so that it is displayed in alphabetical order of **Surname**.

9. Type **TOTAL** in **D24** and show the total number of days absence in **E24**. What is the total value?

10. Type **AVERAGE** in **D25** and show the average number of days absence in **E26**. Format the cell as numeric with 2 decimal places. What is the average value?

11. Save the workbook as **Absences** and close it.

General Exercises

The following revision exercises can involve processes from any part of the ECDL advanced syllabus.

General Exercises

Advanced Revision Exercises

Exercise 35

1. Open the workbook **Supplies** and display the **Orders** sheet.

2. Freeze rows **1** to **4** of the worksheet.

3. The order values have been calculated so the **Price** and **Quantity** columns are not needed. Hide those 2 columns.

4. Insert a column to the right of **Customer** and label it **Contact**. Make sure it has the same formatting as the other headers.

5. Use a lookup function in **H5** in the new column, to display the name of the contact for the **Print Shop**. The names of the contacts for each customer are listed in a table on the **Customer** sheet of the workbook. Copy the lookup function to the range **H6:H49**.

6. We need to know who is buying what. Create a Pivot table based on all of the orders data and place it on a new sheet. Use **Customer** as the row field, **Product** as the column field and total **Value** as the data field. According to the table, which is the only customer not to buy cartridges?

7. Rename the new sheet as **Pivot** and apply an **AutoFormat** of **Table 8**.

8. On the **Orders** sheet, sort the list by **Customer** in ascending order then by **Date** in ascending order.

9. Display subtotals on the list so that total value for every customer is displayed after the orders for each customer.

10. On the **Orders** sheet, use an advanced filter to produce a new list of all orders dated before November 2003 that have not yet been paid. Use rows 2 and 3 for the selection criteria and place the new list at cell **A62**.

11. Add a function in **F75** to show the total value of this list. Add the following comment to that cell; **This debt is more than 2 months overdue and needs to be chased NOW**.

12. Use a database function in **F59** to show the total value of orders in the main list for the last quarter of 2003 (dates on or after the 1st October).

Revision Series
© CiA Training Ltd 2005

13. On the **Sales** sheet, the figure for the last quarter sales value is missing. Create a link here to the contents of **F59** on the **Orders** sheet.

14. On the chart, change the chart type for the sales data to be **2D clustered column**. Decrease the gap width for the columns to **50**.

15. Change the font for the labels on both axes to be **9pt** and **Bold**.

16. Save the workbook as **Supplies2** and close it.

Exercise 36

1. Open the template **NextYear**.

2. Save the file as a **Microsoft Excel Workbook** named **Forecast2004**. This workbook will forecast the operating result for a small hotel, based largely on the figures from the previous year.

3. Switch to the **Rooms** sheet and import data from the text file **Rooms.txt**. This shows the room occupancy figures from 2003. The data is tab delimited and should be inserted at cell **A2**.

4. Switch to the **Costs** sheet and import data from the text file **Costs.txt**. This shows the estimated cost figures for 2004. The data is tab delimited and should be inserted at cell **A2**.

5. Copy the range **B3:M10** from the **Costs** sheet and paste it into **B10** on the **Forecast** sheet so that links are pasted rather than the actual values.

6. Define names for each of the cells in the range **B21:B25** on the **Forecast** sheet. The names should be **B21 - Single**, **B22 - Double**, **B23 - Family**, **B24 - Suite** and **B25 - Increase**.

7. Add a formula in **B4** to calculate the forecast revenue from single rooms in January. Use names wherever possible. The calculation is;

    The Single room rate (from the **Forecast** sheet), multiplied by

    Last years occupancy (from the **Rooms** sheet) multiplied by

    The expected increase level (1 + the **Occupancy Increase** percent)

8. Copy the formula to the range **C4:M4**. If the formula is entered correctly it will copy successfully.

9. Similarly enter formulas to calculate the forecast revenue for Double rooms, Family rooms and the Conference suite. Because the necessary calculations were present on the template, the spreadsheet should be complete.

10. Create a scenario where the changing cells are **B21:B25**. Use the existing values and name the scenario **Mean**.

11. Create another two scenarios with the following values;

Cheap	**B21**	**£25**
	B22	**£40**
	B23	**£50**
	B24	**£700**
	B25	**0.2**

    (Lower prices, higher growth)

Pricey	**B21**	**£35**
	B22	**£50**
	B23	**£60**
	B24	**£800**
	B25	**0.0**

    (Higher prices, zero growth)

12. Produce a scenario summary on a separate sheet within the workbook, based on the three scenarios defined. The results cell is **N19**. Print a copy of the summary sheet.

13. Create a simple pie chart based on the values in cells **N4:N7** of the **Forecast** sheet. Call the chart **Revenue by Room Type** and create it on a separate sheet called **Chart**.

14. Show **Category name** and **Percentage** (**Label and percent** in *Excel97*) as data labels and remove the **Legend**.

15. Change the chart type to **Exploded Pie** chart with 3D effect. Change the **Title** to **14pt** and print a copy of the chart.

16. Protect all the cells on the **Forecast** sheet except the range **B21:B25**.

17. Can cell **B3** be changed? Can cell **B24** be changed?

18. Save the workbook as **Forecast2004** and close it.

Exercise 37

1. Open the workbook **Commission** showing the sales figures for the sales personnel in the various regions of the Big Teeth Software company. The workbook is password protected and requires a password of **pass** to open it.

2. Define names of **Hit** and **Miss** for the possible commission rates in **C32** and **C33**.

3. In **H5** enter a formula to calculate the sales commission to pay. The conditions are that if sales have equalled or exceeded the target, then the commission is the sales value multiplied by the **On Target** percentage. Where sales are less than target, commission is the sales value multiplied by the **Below Target** percentage. Use the defined cell names in the formula and copy the formula to the range **H6:H27**.

4. Format the figures in column **H** as **Currency** with no decimal places.

5. Apply conditional formatting to the figures in column **H** so that values over £5000 are shown in bold with a pale yellow background and values less than £1000 are shown in red font.

6. In **I5** enter a formula to calculate the approximate age of the salesperson. Use an expression which subtracts the **Date of Birth** value from the date on the worksheet shown in **D1**, and divides by **365**.

7. Include a function display the value in **I5** as the next highest whole number (no decimal places). Apply the formula to the range **I6:I27** and make sure the format is numeric with no decimal places.

8. Sort the data, first by **Region** (ascending) then by **Sales** (descending).

9. Apply subtotals so that the average **Sales** and **Age** is shown below the data for each **Region**. Which regions have an average sales value greater than their target? Which region has the highest average age of salesperson?

10. Everyone over **40** next birthday, with a sales figure of less than **£175000** is to be retrained. Apply an advanced filter (use rows 2 and 3 for the criteria) to create a new list of people who meet these conditions, starting in **A40**. How many are there?

11. Change the display of the main sorted list so that only the **Region** subtotals are shown.

12. Produce a 2D Pie chart based on the subtotal values and their labels. Give it a title of **Sales by Region**, and create it on a new sheet called **Sales Chart**.

13. Format the chart to show **Category name** and **Percentage** (**Label and percent** in *Excel97*) as data labels and remove the **Legend**. Format the Title as **18pt**.

14. Move the **Data Labels** into the appropriate chart segments. If any segment is too dark to show the text, reformat that segment only with a lighter colour.

15. Change the angle of the first slice so that the segment for the **Southern** region is shown at the top of the chart.

16. Change the chart type to an **Exploded Pie** chart.

17. Print a copy of the **Sales Chart** sheet.

18. Save the workbook as **Averages**, removing the password protection before it is saved, then close it.

Exercise 38

1. Open the workbook **Storage**. A worksheet showing the results for a small engineering company making storage tanks has been set up but needs amending.

2. Every cell on the **Results** sheet is locked and password protection has been applied. Remove the protection for the sheet. The password is **tanks**.

3. It is suspected that there is an error in the calculations in column **G**. Trace the precedents of the cells **G3:G5** to determine the problem.

4. Correct the error and trace the precedents for the corrected cell again. Select and print the range **A1:G12** showing the (correct) precedents for **G3:G5**, then remove all arrows from the sheet.

5. Enter a formula in **G8** to check the total margin. Do this by adding together the results of multiplying the totals sold for each size tank (**F3:F5**) by the individual margin for that size tank (**B10:B12**). The margin values have been given names, use them in the formula.

6. Format **G3:G8** as **Currency** with no decimal places.

7. On the chart, add a title of **Margin by Tank Size** and do not show the **Legend**.

8. Amend the **Source Data** for the chart so that the **Category (X) Axis** is based on the text in **A3:A5**. Format the text on both axes to be **Times New Roman**, **10pt**, **bold**.

General Exercises

9. Format the data series columns so that they contain pictures. Use the image **Tank** from the supplied files and specify a **Stacked** format.

10. Switch to the **Calculator** sheet to complete the table showing the volume of storage tanks based on their height and radius. The formula for the volume is entered in **B6** but is showing an **Error**. Define the necessary names in **C2** and **C3** to correct the error.

11. Create a two input data table in **B6:H12** based on the calculation in **B6**. Format **C7:H12** to be **Numeric** with 2 decimal places.

12. Hide rows **2** and **3**.

13. Apply conditional formatting to the range **C7:H12** so that all volumes greater than 100 cu metres are shown in red, bold and italic.

14. Add another condition to the formatting so that volumes less than 15 are shown as green and italic.

15. Create a macro that will prepare this sheet for printout. It should change the page orientation to **Landscape**, set the left and right margins to 1.4, centre the spreadsheet vertically and horizontally and set **Gridlines** to be included. Name the macro **Prepare** and store it with the current workbook only.

16. Switch to the results sheet and display the worksheet showing formula rather than values. Print out the first page of the worksheet.

17. Save the workbook as **Complete** and close it.

Exercise 39

1. Open the workbook **Register**. This shows the attendance records relating to an 8 week IT course.

2. Using the **Register** sheet, freeze the top two rows and the first column from the left.

3. In column **N**, use a function to display the average attendance for each student. Format the cells as **Percentage**, with 2 decimal places.

4. Use a nested function in cell **O3** to create a code consisting of the first three characters of the student's **Surname** in upper case, added to their **Student No**. For example the code for the first student should be **WAL101**. The functions to use are **CONCATENATE**, **LEFT** and **UPPER**.

5. Copy the formula to the range **O4:O28**.

6. Open the workbook **ITgrades**. This shows the final grades for students on this course. Copy the grades from **ITgrades** and paste them as linked values into the range **P3:P28** of **Register**.

7. Centre align the contents of column **P**.

8. Sort the data (**A2:P28** including headers) first by **M/F** then by **Surname**.

9. Add subtotals to show the average attendance for **Females** and **Males**. Show the subtotals below the data.

10. Add further subtotals (without replacing the current ones) to show the minimum attendance for **Females** and **Males**.

11. Starting in **B37**, create the following area.

	A	B	C	D	E
35					
36					
37		Female			
38					
39		No of A grades			
40		No of B grades			
41		No of C grades			
42					

12. Use **COUNTIF** functions in **D39:D41** to count the number of **A, B** and **C** grades. Make sure all functions just refer to the data range for females, ie rows **3** to **14**.

13. Create a similar area for the male data, starting in **B44**. Make sure all functions just refer to the data range for males, i.e. rows **17** to **30**.

14. Highlight **A35:E50** and print only this section of the spreadsheet.

15. Copy the grades from **ITgrades** workbook again and paste them as values (not linked) into column **F** of the **Details** sheet.

General Exercises

16. Use date functions in columns **G** and **H** of the **Details** sheet to shown the **Month** and **Year** from the **Date of Birth** field.

17. Use **Autofilter** to show the students born in month 9. How many are there?

18. Remove the **Autofilter** and create a Pivot table from the data in the **Details** sheet. Use **Year** as the row field, **Grade** as the column field and number of **Surnames** as the data. Create the table on a separate sheet named **Table**.

19. Group the **Year** data into 1960's, 1970,s and 1980's. Name the grouping as **Decade** and name the groups **60's**, **70's** and **80's**.

20. Hide the detail so that only the decade values are shown. Print the table without further formatting.

21. Save the workbook as **Statistics** and close it.

22. Close the **ITgrades** workbook <u>without</u> saving.

Answers

This section contains answers to all specific questions posed in the preceding exercises, together with the name of the file or files containing the worked solution for each exercise.

Answers

Advanced Revision Exercises

Exercise 1

Step 7   The total net profit changes to **£21,442.00**.

A sample solution for this exercise is saved as **Results2 Solution.xls** in the **Spreadsheet Solutions** folder.

Exercise 2

A sample solution for this exercise is saved as **Results2 Solution.xls** in the **Spreadsheet Solutions** folder. The finished spreadsheet should look similar to the one below.

Head Office Employees

No	Surname	First	Department	Salary	Date of Birth	Length of Service
1	Parke	Neil	Marketing	£22,200	30-Dec-62	8
2	Patel	Ravinder	Marketing	£15,200	24-Feb-50	10
3	Chesterton	Ian	Training	£24,000	5-May-55	12
4	Smith	David	Finance	£28,200	10-Apr-66	5
5	Waldram	Zara	Computer Services	£19,800	1-Mar-67	4
6	Smith	James	Development	£14,400	27-Nov-81	2
7	Waterman	David	Computer Services	£17,400	12-Jun-68	3
8	Smith	John	Development	£14,400	17-Oct-59	1
9	Westgarth	Shaun	Catering	£13,200	13-Jan-67	2
10	McMillan	Rose	Development	£16,200	22-Jul-54	5
11	Wright	Margaret	Training	£12,000	27-Sep-55	3
12	Zapora	Androv	Catering	£10,800	18-Feb-61	6
13	Yates	Zeta	Personnel	£15,600	8-May-63	4
14	Li	Anna	Computer Services	£21,600	12-May-61	9
15	Borland	James	Administration	£18,000	21-Sep-49	8
16	Clarke	Amy	Marketing	£22,200	13-Jul-73	6
17	Singh	Vikram	Personnel	£16,200	31-Dec-50	12
18	Oman	Tariq	Administration	£21,600	17-Apr-73	4

Revision Series
© CiA Training Ltd 2005

Exercise 3

Step 8   The change is allowed. The net pay changes to **£265.60**.

Step 9   The change is not allowed. A warning message is displayed.

Step 10   The **Unhide** option is not available on the menu.

Step 11   The worksheet protection would have to be removed.

Step 12   A sample solution for this exercise is saved as **Secure2 Solution.xls** in the **Spreadsheet Solutions** folder.

Exercise 4

Step 2   Select **Format | Sheet** and the **Unhide** option will be available. Or
Look at the formula in **C5** for example. It refers to data from another worksheet.

Step 7   **Yes**. The protection is only against directly entered changes.

Step 10   Enter a password for full access or open the workbook as read only.

Step 12   **Yes** data entry is still allowed.

Step 13   **No**. The workbook cannot be saved under its original name, as this would be an update.

A sample solution for this exercise is saved as **Cars2 Solution.xls** in the **Spreadsheet Solutions** folder.

Exercise 5

A sample solution for this exercise is saved as **Business2 Solution.xls** in the **Spreadsheet Solutions** folder.

Exercise 6

Step 4   **View | Comments**

Answers

Step 8

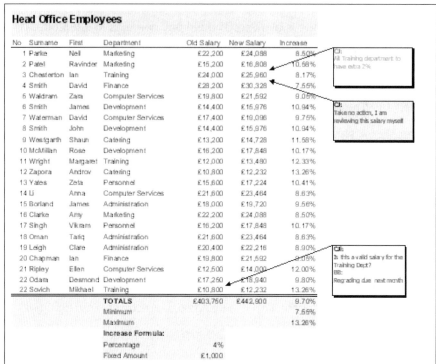

A sample solution for this exercise is saved as **Wages2 Solution.xls** in the **Spreadsheet Solutions** folder.

Exercise 7

Step 4   =Hourly_Rate*Normal_Hours

Step 5   =IF(Gross_Pay<50,0,(Gross_Pay-50)*NI)

Step 6   £230

Step 7   =Basic_Pay Fisher

Step 11   =Gross_Pay*Pension

Step 12   £110

A sample solution for this exercise is saved as **Payroll2 Solution.xls** in the **Spreadsheet Solutions** folder.

Exercise 8

Step 4   **=E3*(1+Rate)**

Step 7   **=Apr*(1+Rate)**

Step 8   **=SUM((Wages May):(Overheads May))**

Step 10 **Total**

A sample solution for this exercise is saved as **Growth2 Solution.xls** in the **Spreadsheet Solutions** folder.

Exercise 9

Step 7   Total pay is **£195**

A sample solution for this exercise is saved as **Timesheet Solution.xls** in the **Spreadsheet Solutions** folder.

Exercise 10

Step 12 **Net Profit** is **50,029**.

A sample solution for this exercise is saved as **Plan2 Solution.xls** in the **Spreadsheet Solutions** folder.

Exercise 11

Step 2   In the formula in **G6**, the reference **D6** refers to a non numeric cell. This should be **E6**.

Step 3   In the formula in **G10**, a character **o** is used in a cell reference instead of a numeric zero. The correct reference should be **F10**.

Step 4   The values for **Department** and **Old Salary** have been reversed, resulting in an invalid calculation. Switch the two values around

Step 5   The errors in the total calculations are only due to invalid values in the individual rows. Once these are corrected, the errors in the total calculations will be automatically removed.

Answers

Step 6   The custom number format should be entered as **000-000**.

A sample solution for this exercise is saved as **Office2 Solution.xls** in the **Spreadsheet Solutions** folder.

Exercise 12

Step 2   In the formulas in **C8** and **D8**, the second term in the division should be **E7** in both cases.

Step 3   The most likely cause for these errors is by copying the formula in **B8** without making the **E7** reference absolute.

Step 4   In the formula in **B13**, the reference to **A10** should be **B10**. The error in **E13** is due to cell **B13** not being defined. Correcting **B13** will automatically correct **E13**.

Step 5   **ddd dd mmm yyyy**

Step 7

Bob's Barrow				
Fruit	Apples	Pears	Oranges	Total
Jan	36	38	26	=SUM(B4:D4)
Feb	40	26	37	=SUM(B5:D5)
Mar	53	23	84	=SUM(B6:D6)
Total	=SUM(B4:B6)	=SUM(C4:C6)	=SUM(D4:D6)	=SUM(B7:D7)
Percentage	=B7/E7	=C7/E7	=D7/E7	
Retail Price	15	17	16	
Income	=B7*B10	=C7*C10	=D7*D10	=SUM(B11:D11)
Wholesale Price	10	11	11	
Net Profit	=(B10-B12)*B7	=(C10-C12)*C7	=(D10-D12)*D7	=SUM(B13:D13)
Prepared on: 38094				

A sample solution for this exercise is saved as **Fruit2 Solution.xls** in the **Spreadsheet Solutions** folder.

Exercise 13

Step 7   The **Cheap** scenario results in the biggest loss (**-33,943**).

A sample solution for this exercise is saved as **Company2 Solution.xls** in the **Spreadsheet Solutions** folder. The scenario summary should look similar to this.

Scenario Summary						
	Current Values:	Base	Bad News	Recovery	Cheap	Hopeful
Changing Cells:						
$B$15	3%	5%	3%	3%	8%	8%
$B$16	7.2	7	7	7.2	6.5	7
Result Cells:						
$N$12	8,037	1,158	-8,993	8,037	-33,943	22,988

Exercise 14

Step 5 **High rate**

Step 7 The greatest spread is in the **High Amount** scenario. The spread is **7.43%**.

A sample solution for this exercise is saved as **NewSalaries2 Solution.xls** in the **Spreadsheet Solutions** folder. The scenario summary should look similar to this.

Scenario Summary				
	Current Values:	Medium	High Amount	High Rate
Changing Cells:				
Percentage	4%	4%	2%	6%
Fixed	£1,000	£1,000	£1,300	£500
Result Cells:				
Overall	9.70%	9.70%	9.41%	8.85%
Minimum	7.55%	7.55%	6.61%	7.77%
Maximum	13.26%	13.26%	14.04%	10.63%

Exercise 15

Step 2 **=C4*Central!C5**

Step 3 **=C6*Central!C6**

Step 4 **=Central!C7**

Step 6 **Oldfield, -63,676**

Step 7 **=SUM(Newtown:Concord!C12), 127,818**

Step 8 **99,758**

A sample solution for this exercise is saved as **Bits2 Solution.xls** in the **Spreadsheet Solutions** folder.

Answers

Exercise 16

Step 4   **Family Rooms**, **53.8%**

Step 6

The Three Horseshoes Inn   **Annual Report**

2003 Occupancy

This page shows the occupancy figures for the year 2003

2003	Single Rooms	Double Rooms	Twin Rooms	Family Rooms
Maximum	1800	3600	2160	1080
Actual	1006	2332	1352	581
Percentage	55.89%	64.78%	62.59%	53.80%

Step 14   A sample solution for this exercise is saved as **Horseshoes2 Solution.xls** in the **Spreadsheet Solutions** folder.

Exercise 17

Step 2   **Descending**

Step 3   **James Borland**

Step 4   **Anna Li**

Step 6   **£71,300**.

Step 7   **3** years average for **Development**, **5** years for the **Company**.

A sample solution for this exercise is saved as **Staff2 Solution.xls** in the **Spreadsheet Solutions** folder. The final spreadsheet should look similar to this.

1 2 3		A	B	C	D	E	F	G
	1	Head Office Employees						
	2							
	3	No	Surname	First	Department	Salary	Date of Birth	Length of Service
+	7				Administration Average			5
+	10				Catering Average			4
+	15				Computer Services Average			5
+	20				Development Average			3
·	21	20	Chapman	Ian	Finance	£19,800	12-May-61	7
·	22	4	Smith	David	Finance	£28,200	10-Apr-66	5
−	23				Finance Average			6
+	27				Marketing Average			8
+	30				Personnel Average			8
+	34				Training Average			5
−	35				Company Average			5

Exercise 18

A sample solution for this exercise is saved as **Events2 Solution.xls** in the **Spreadsheet Solutions** folder.

Exercise 19

Step 4   **9** items

Step 5   **5** items

Step 6   **5** items

Step 8

Order Form

Code	Type	Item	Stock Quantity	Weekly Turnover	Weeks Stock	Order Quantity
B004	Beers	Ambrosia Brown Ale	33	40	0.83	100
B002	Beers	Berbs Bitter (large)	42	150	0.28	300
B006	Beers	Sunset Lager	24	75	0.32	150

A sample solution for this exercise is saved as **Stock2 Solution.xls** in the **Spreadsheet Solutions** folder.

Answers

Exercise 20

Step 2   **4**

Step 3   **2**

Step 4   **7**

Step 5   **4**

Step 6   **12**

A sample solution for this exercise is saved as **Employees2 Solution.xls** in the **Spreadsheet Solutions** folder. The final spreadsheet should look similar to this.

Head Office Employees							
No	Surname	First	Department	Salary	Salary	Date of Birth	Length of Service
				>=15000	<=20000		>5
						<01/01/64	
No	Surname	First	Department	Salary	Date of Birth	Length of Service	
1	Parke	Neil	Marketing	£22,200	30-Dec-62	8	
2	Patel	Ravinder	Marketing	£15,200	24-Feb-50	10	
3	Chesterton	Ian	Training	£24,000	5-May-55	12	
8	Smith	John	Development	£14,400	17-Oct-59	1	
10	McMillan	Rose	Development	£16,200	22-Jul-54	5	
11	Wright	Margaret	Training	£12,000	27-Sep-55	3	
12	Zapora	Androv	Catering	£10,800	18-Feb-61	6	
13	Yates	Zeta	Personnel	£15,600	8-May-63	4	
14	Li	Anna	Computer Services	£21,600	12-May-61	9	
15	Borland	James	Administration	£18,000	21-Sep-49	8	
17	Singh	Vikram	Personnel	£16,200	31-Dec-50	12	
20	Chapman	Ian	Finance	£19,800	12-May-61	7	

Exercise 21

Step 5   **4**

Step 8   **5**

Step 12   A sample solution for this exercise is saved as **Analysis2 Solution.xls** in the **Spreadsheet Solutions** folder.

Revision Series
© CiA Training Ltd 2005

Exercise 22

Step 3

Type	Weekly Turnover
Alcopops	270
Beers	567
Foods	242
Miscellaneous	260
Sodas	200
Spirits	30
Wines	142
Grand Total	1711

A sample solution for this exercise is saved as **Goods2 Solution.xls** in the **Spreadsheet Solutions** folder. The sample final pivot table was formatted in *Excel XP* with **Table 4 AutoFormat** and should look similar to this.

Count of Item		Type						
Weekly Turnove	Weekly Turnover	Alcopops	Beers	Foods	Sodas	Spirits	Wines	Grand Total
1-10			2	1		8	4	15
11-50		9	3	5	5		6	28
51-100			2	1	1			4
Over 100			2					2
Grand Total		9	9	7	6	8	10	49

Exercise 23

Step 4   Sum = **252,350**, count = **12**

Step 5   Sum = **151,300**, count = **11**

Step 9   **=HLOOKUP(G4,$E$34:$G$35,2,TRUE)**. The TRUE parameter is optional.

Step 12   **=IF(E4>1700,E4*0.04,E4*0.05)**

Step 14   **25** days holiday, **£864** salary increase

Answers

Step 15 A sample solution for this exercise is saved as **Holidays2 Solution.xls** in the **Spreadsheet Solutions** folder.

Exercise 24

Step 6 **21, =DCOUNT(A4:H49,1,A2:H3)**. Note that the criteria range could be replaced with **G2:H3** for the same result. **DCOUNTA** counts non numeric cells and could have been used with text columns **4**, **5** or **6**.

Step 7 **£13,672**

Step 8 **17** and **£8,985**

Step 9 **=IF(AND(G5=FALSE,H5>45),"PAY", " ")**

Step 10 **=CONCATENATE(F5," ",E5)**. An alternative answer is **=F5+" "+E5** is easier but it is not a function and therefore incorrect as an answer to the question.

Step 14 **=Today()**

Step 15 A sample solution for this exercise is saved as **Debts2 Solution.xls** in the **Spreadsheet Solutions** folder.

Exercise 25

Step 6

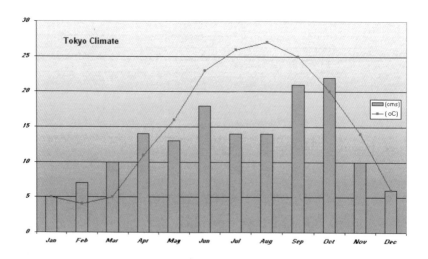

Revision Series
© CiA Training Ltd 2005

Step 11

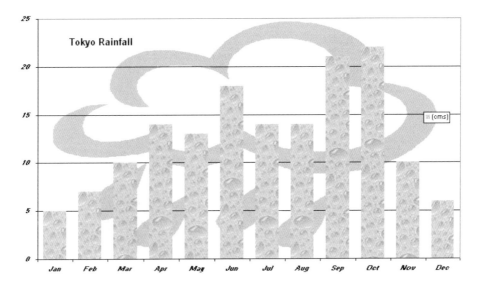

Step 13

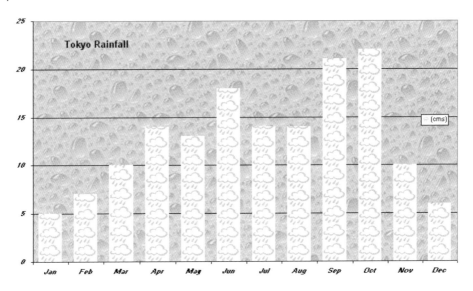

A sample solution for this exercise is saved as **Tokyo2 Solution.xls** in the **Spreadsheet Solutions** folder.

Answers

Advanced Revision Exercises

Exercise 26

Step 11

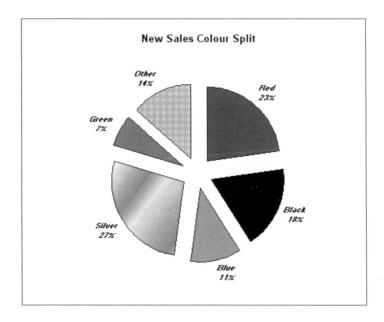

New Sales Colour Split

A sample solution for this exercise is saved as **Sales2 Solution.xls** in the **Spreadsheet Solutions** folder.

Exercise 27

Step 7   Warp Factor **3**

Step 8   **14** crystals

A sample solution for this exercise is saved as **Starship2 Solution.xls** in the **Spreadsheet Solutions** folder.

Exercise 28

Step 9   **17**

Step 10   **£35**

Step 11   **Yes**

Revision Series
© CiA Training Ltd 2005

A sample solution for this exercise is saved as **Minibus Solution**.xls in the **Spreadsheet Solutions** folder.

Exercise 29

Step 9

```
Sub Stamp()
'
' Stamp Macro
' Macro recorded 27/01/2004 by Bob Browell
'
' Keyboard Shortcut: Ctrl+q
'
    Selection.Font.Italic = True
    ActiveCell.FormulaR1C1 = "Property of CiA Training Co"
    Range("C2").Select
End Sub
```

A sample solution for this exercise is saved as **Exercise30**.xls in the **Spreadsheet Solutions** folder.

Exercise 30

Step 13 The macro will be available because it is associated with the workbook, but the button will not be available because it is associated with the *Excel* application and it was deleted in step 10.

A sample solution for this exercise is saved as **Vehicles2 Solution**.xls in the **Spreadsheet Solutions** folder.

Exercise 31

Step 2   **5** cells are circled.

Step 3   The **Formula Auditing** toolbar. It has **12** buttons.

Step 5   They include a reference to a cell in column **D**.

Step 7   **Yes**, there is an arrow pointing to every cell.

Step 10 The error is immediately due to an error in **F27**.

Answers

Advanced Revision Exercises

Step 11   **F27** sums column **F** and there is an error in **F14**.

Step 12

	A	B	C	D	E	F	G	H
13	10	McMillan	Rose	Development	£16,200	£17,848	10.17%	504361
14	11	Wright	Margaret	£12,000	Training	#VALUE!	#VALUE!	495839
15	12	Zapora	Androv	Catering	£10,800	£12,232	13.26%	921976
16	13	Yates	Zeta	Personnel	£15,600	£17,224	10.41%	943354
17	14	Li	Anna	Computer Services	£21,600	£23,464	8.63%	252559
18	15	Borland	James	Administration	£18,000	£19,720	9.56%	628106
19	16	Clarke	Amy	Marketing	£22,200	£24,088	8.50%	20836
20	17	Singh	Vikram	Personnel	£16,200	£17,848	10.17%	181770
21	18	Oman	Tariq	Administration	£21,600	£23,464	8.63%	440015
22	19	Leigh	Clare	Administration	£20,400	£22,216	8.90%	810067
23	20	Chapman	Ian	Finance	£19,800	£21,592	9.05%	616049
24	21	Ripley	Ellen	Computer Services	£12,500	£14,000	12.00%	729765
25	22	Odara	Desmond	Development	£17,250	£18,940	9.80%	708552
26	22	Sovich	Mikhael	Training	£10,800	£12,232	13.26%	510038
27				TOTALS	£391,750	#VALUE!	#VALUE!	
28								
29								
30								
31				Increase Formula:				
32				Percentage		4%		
33				Fixed Amount		£1,000		

A sample solution for this exercise is saved as **Preliminary2 Solution.xls** in the **Spreadsheet Solutions** folder.

Exercise 32

Step 3   The profit calculation on **Oldfield** does not include the Head Office Costs, **C10**.

Step 4   **Yes** the **Production Cost per Unit** is used correctly in **C8** on all sheets.

Step 5   **Overhead Costs per Employee** is only used on two of the sheets. It is not used on **Concord**. Amend the formula in **C9** of the **Concord** sheet to reference **C6** on the Central sheet.

Step 6   The formula for **Consolidated Profit** only includes values from two of the sheets. It does not use the value from **Concord**. Amend the function in **C12** of the **Central** sheet to include the **Concord** sheet, e.g. **=SUM(Newtown:Concord!C12)**

Step 7   **£94,758**.

Revision Series
© CiA Training Ltd 2005

A sample solution for this exercise is saved as **Manufacturing2 Solution.xls** in the **Spreadsheet Solutions** folder.

Exercise 33

Step 8   **£18730.17**

A sample solution for this exercise is saved as **Invoices2 Solution.xls** in the **Spreadsheet Solutions** folder.

Exercise 34

Step 9   **49**

Step 10   **2.23**

A sample solution for this exercise is saved as **Absences Solution.xls** in the **Spreadsheet Solutions** folder.

Exercise 35

Step 5   **=VLOOKUP(G5,Customers!$B$3:$C$9,2,FALSE)**

Step 6   **IT Supplies**

Step 7

Value Customer	Cartridges	CD ROMs	Cleaning Kits	DVDs	Labels	Printer Paper	Screen Filters	Toner	Grand Total
Byte Size	108	220				255.36	179.76	1248	2011.12
IT Supplies		176	958.08			446.88		624	2204.96
Kings	432	264				574.56	359.52		1630.08
Pink Computers	432	132	359.28			766.08	359.52		2048.88
Print Shop	1116			1150.08	310	1244.88		936	4756.96
Tekno	180	1364	479.04	718.8			719.04		3460.88
The IT Store	216	132	239.52	431.28	186		179.76		1384.56
Grand Total	**2484**	**2288**	**2035.92**	**2300.16**	**496**	**3287.76**	**1797.6**	**2808**	**17497.44**

Step 12   **£12,189.68**

Step 15

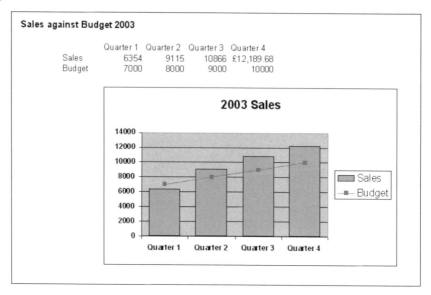

A sample solution for this exercise is saved as **Analysis Solution.xls** in the **Spreadsheet Solutions** folder.

Exercise 36

Step 7   **=Single*Rooms!B3*(1+Increase)**

Step 12

Scenario Summary				
	Current Values:	Mean	Cheap	Pricey
Changing Cells:				
Single	£30.00	£30.00	£25.00	£35.00
Double	£45.00	£45.00	£40.00	£50.00
Family	£55.00	£55.00	£50.00	£60.00
Suite	£750.00	£750.00	£700.00	£800.00
Increase	10%	10%	20%	0%
Result Cells:				
$N$19	£73,501.43	£73,501.43	£64,146.43	£77,759.43

Notes: Current Values column represents values of changing cells at time Scenario Summary Report was created. Changing cells for each scenario are highlighted in gray.

Step 15

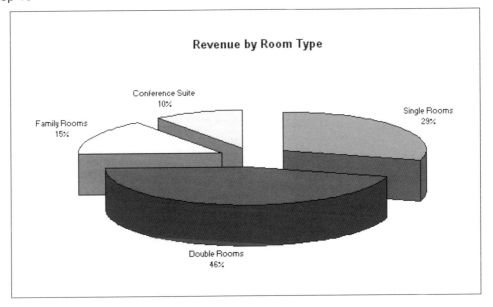

Step 17 **B3** <u>cannot</u> be changed, it is a protected cell. **B24** <u>can</u> be changed, it is an unprotected cell.

A sample solution for this exercise is saved as **Forecast2004 Solution**.**xls** in the **Spreadsheet Solutions** folder.

Exercise 37

Step 3 **=IF(E5>=F5,E5*Hit,E5*Miss)**

Step 7 **=ROUNDUP(($D$1-G5)/365,0)**

Step 9 **Northern** and **Southern** averages are above target, **Eastern** has the highest average age.

Step 10 **3** people

Step 17 For this chart to be displayed correctly, the **Data** worksheet must be shown summarised, i.e. region averages only.

Answers

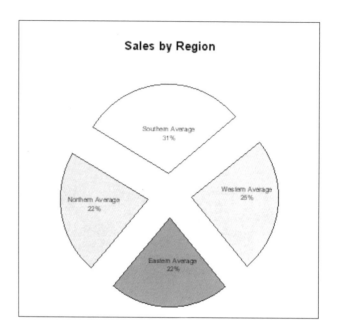

A sample solution for this exercise is saved as **Averages Solution.xls** in the **Spreadsheet Solutions** folder.

Exercise 38

Step 4

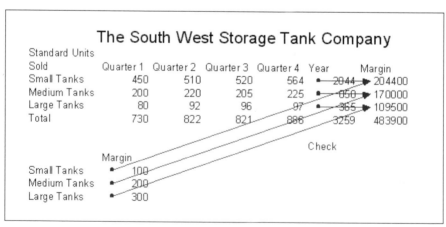

Step 5   **=F3*Small+F4*Medium+F5*Large**

Step 9

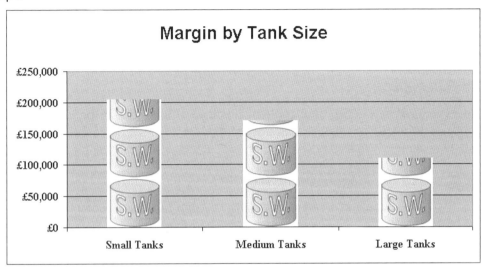

A sample solution for this exercise is saved as **Complete Solution.xls** in the **Spreadsheet Solutions** folder.

Exercise 39

Step 4   **=CONCATENATE(LEFT(UPPER(B3),3),A3)**

Step 17 **5** people born in month **9**

Step 19

Count of Surname		Grade			
Decade	Year	A	B	C	Grand Total
60's		3	5	1	9
70's		3	3	2	8
80's		3	4	2	9
Grand Total		9	12	5	26

A sample solution for this exercise is saved as **Statistics Solution.xls** in the **Spreadsheet Solutions** folder.

Answers

Other Products from CiA Training

If you have enjoyed using this guide you can obtain other products from our range of over 150 titles. CiA Training Ltd is a leader in developing self-teach training materials and courseware.

Open Learning Guides

Teach yourself by working through them in your own time. Our range includes products for: Windows, Word, Excel, Access, PowerPoint, Project, Publisher, Internet Explorer, FrontPage and many more... We also have a large back catalogue of products; please call for details.

ECDL/ICDL

We produce accredited training materials for the European Computer Driving Licence (ECDL/ICDL) and the Advanced ECDL/ICDL qualifications. The standard level consists of seven modules and the advanced level four modules. Material produced covers a variety of Microsoft Office products from Office 97 to 2003.

e-Citizen

Courseware for this exciting new qualification is available now. Students will become proficient Internet users and participate confidently in all major aspects of the online world with the expert guidance of this handbook. Simulated web sites are also supplied for safe practice before tackling the real thing.

New CLAiT, CLAiT Plus and CLAiT Advanced

Open learning publications are now available for the new OCR CLAiT 2006 qualifications. The publications enable the user to learn the features needed to pass the assessments using a gradual step by step approach.

Trainer's Packs

Specifically written for use with tutor led I.T. courses. The trainer is supplied with a trainer guide (step by step exercises), course notes (for delegates), consolidation exercises (for use as reinforcement) and course documents (course contents, pre-course questionnaires, evaluation forms, certificate template, etc). All supplied on CD with rights to edit and copy the documents.

Online Shop

To purchase or browse the CiA catalogue please visit, *www.ciatraining.co.uk*.